ORION'S BELT AT THE END OF THE DRIVE

Orion's Belt at the End of the Drive

Poems by
Pat Williams Owen

Accents Publishing • Lexington, Kentucky • 2019

Copyright © 2019 by Pat Williams Owen
All rights reserved

Printed in the United States of America

Accents Publishing
Editor: Katerina Stoykova

Library of Congress Control Number: 2019933965
ISBN: 978-1-936628-47-6
First Edition

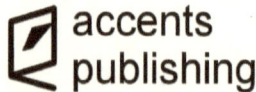

Accents Publishing is an independent press for brilliant voices. For a catalog of current and upcoming titles, please visit us on the Web at

www.accents-publishing.com

CONTENTS

Orion's Belt at the End of the Drive / 1
Old Fashioned Child Portrait / 2
Blood / 3
Against the Backdrop / 4
Human-Tender / 5
Single Gentleman / 6
Marriage of Academics / 7
The Poetry Critique / 8
The Creature / 9
The Tin Man / 10
The Discipline of the Dancer / 11
Asperger Musician / 12
Small Gestures / 13
The Wild Raw Green of Kentucky / 14
The Peruvian Zumba Teacher / 15
Completion / 17
My Dentist / 18
To Be Female / 19
Cervix / 20
A Young Lesbian Couple / 21
Middle-Aged Couple / 22
Old Flame / 23
Wrinkles / 25
Longing for Hale-Bopp / 26
Ink / 27
Confirmation / 28
Unattainable / 29
Refrain / 30
At Cross Country Meet / 32
From My Porch in the High Rise / 33
Summer Solstice II / 34
The Otter / 35
Pedestrians / 36
Cave Hill Once Again / 37
Self-Care / 38

Meditations on the Vietnam Wall / 39
College Baseball Team on the Plane / 40
Boarding School at Pebble Beach / 41
Reification / 42
Elkhorn Fern / 43
Sapling / 44
Cottonwood Tree / 45
After My Untimely Death / 46

About the Author / 49

*Let each day sit
on its own bottom,
unburdened with the past,
sufficient unto its self.*

ORION'S BELT AT THE END OF THE DRIVE

So many years I went out to get the paper
early in the dark
breathing in the night sky,
my one brief contemplation of infinity
for the day
and if there was a full moon,
I would open my arms to it
and bow,
aligning myself, my place in the universe
by the stars.

OLD FASHIONED CHILD PORTRAIT

Pigtails braided tight and tied
on top of the head with a bow.
It hurt to get it that way,
twisted and pulled with a yank,
everything in control.
A gold heart locket
and lace around the collar.
Eyes tender and trusting
in this three-year-old.

She started biting her nails
so she didn't have to submit
to severe scissor trimming.
She liked the way the nail
slivers felt in her mouth,
discrete and sharp.

BLOOD

I'm always surprised how it appears
bright and fresh on my fingertip.
It seems to spring from a secret
inner pool. I imagine it flowing
through my body, an underground
stream. At the doctor's office, I look
away as they draw dark red tubes
from the plump vein in my right arm.
Once I fainted at the sight of a paper cut
and awoke with people standing around
observing me on the floor.
I knew I'd entered a new realm
with blood on my pants at 13.
Red reality like a matador's cape.

AGAINST THE BACKDROP

On a hard bench in the Cineplex lobby
brightly lit, cavernous,
two women alone in the holiday crowd,
one weeping as though her world is lost,
the other holding, comforting her.
It was years ago, but still
I can't forget the sight.
Against a raucous backdrop of concession lines,
mothers with kids, teenagers laughing—
why did this scene catch my eye?
They could have been sisters, lovers,
friends. Whatever pain was endured,
it must have been eased
by this tenderness.
Now, every time I give comfort
or am comforted, that image
reappears. Is it worth the pain
to be held in this consolation?

HUMAN-TENDER

The sky is streaked with pink
and so the water below.

Lately I've felt more of a tenderness
toward myself. I take pity
on my humanness.

It's such a luxury to live only in the present
moment. It makes everything simple,
easy, hardly anything to do but be.

Everyone I know is so tender and human,
I could just hug and comfort them.
It takes one to know one.

SINGLE GENTLEMAN

He's built like a fireplug—
short and stocky, close to the ground.
He wears busy plaid jackets
and a wide smile
and a Ha, Ha laugh.
He tells me he sleeps in the buff
with his two cats—
hands me his phone to see a pic.
I see two long-haired Persians
with his head in the middle.
On anti-depressants,
he doesn't drink.
His mother and cats—
growing old.

All the papers on his desk—
neatly stacked,
his next trip with his mother—
planned.

MARRIAGE OF ACADEMICS

Books surround them, towering over
and around them. Their library fenced
with walls of books along with overstuffed
chairs, reading lamps.

These walls haven't saved them from
trips to the hospital, surgery,
the fragile rigidity of bodies.

We grapple for protection, a crutch
against the ticking of the clock.

THE POETRY CRITIQUE

The poet shrinks under the attack,
his body curls into withdrawal,
shoulders folded over vulnerable belly.
His torso embodies pain,
scooting lower in his seat,
he tries to disappear.

And still the attacks rain down,
the assailant ranting on without
looking at his victim,
holding forth in his sureness,
oblivious to the wounds.

The lion is unaware of the suffering
of the gazelle.

THE CREATURE

There's a tattered creature
tethered to me
near as my breath
who, thoughtless and callous,
inflicts pain without remorse.
No matter how often I shine it up,
its tarnished nature creeps through.
I try to keep it behind me
out of sight,
pretending it doesn't belong to me
enchained,
though I do see a family resemblance.
Like Pigpen, it's trailed by a cloud of dust.

THE TIN MAN

Does the Tin Man shut down
to protect himself or
was there no heart to start with?
Was there such early damage,
the connecting synapses explode?
Did stoniness live
in his parents even
before he appeared?
If he tries hard can he pass
for normal,
or can people always hear
the clank when he walks?

THE DISCIPLINE OF THE DANCER

The thought of a doughnut
makes him nauseous
even as his friend announces
Krispy Kreme has a giveaway.
The dancer munches an apple
with peanut butter for dinner.
Movement is his drug of choice.
At a party, while others eat
with abandon, he sits removed,
serene and erect,
a slight smile on his face.

ASPERGER MUSICIAN

Hunched over at the piano
nodding his head up and down,

he tries to embody passion.
Tapping his foot, squinting

his eyes, his fingers pound
the keys, his whole frame

reaching for ecstasy.
His head moves back

and forth, so focused
saliva brims at his lips

thin and soft as they are.

SMALL GESTURES

The kindness of the nurse
placing her hand on my arm
during the exam
my gratitude.

Sometimes it takes so little
to show someone you care,
a small effort of kindness
a lifeline to the drowning.

My friend calls her daughters
"my angels" but isn't that
what everyone is for us,
those who are there, caring
watching over us?

I register sadness
because my uterus gave way.
What about Shadow, the Husky,
who has no remaining eyes?
She has to learn to see
with her heart.

THE WILD RAW GREEN OF KENTUCKY

After the tropics
there's a wild raw wind here
cutting through my shirt.
The world's so proud when it's sunny
as though anything is possible
after so much rain.
Maple limbs sway
just as they did
centuries ago
for my forebearers.

THE PERUVIAN ZUMBA TEACHER

I watch her feet like someone learning
a new language. Red flames lap
up the sides of her black tights. Plump
lips, beckoning hands, her tongue

trills the "R" in bravo in a way
foreign to gringo blood. She's so hot
her boyfriend is twenty years younger.
The door of the studio vibrates

with Latin rhythm, calls to all
who will listen, sound reverberating
through the body strong and sure
as a heartbeat. Even on a good day,

no one would mistake me for Latin,
but the class has loosened me up,
made me more daring. I'm trading
my Anglo genes for throbbing Hispanic.

The teacher wants us to shout out
aowl—raw and sexual—
demands it of us good girls
white and professionally proper.

Butt out, Ladies, Shake it!

I follow the teacher's hips
sinuous, gyrating—the tattoos
just below the midriff beckoning
all voyeurs. She will take you down paths

that would make your mother blush.
My small pride at my progress quickly

deflated when at the end of Monday's class
she says to me

You'll be better Friday.

COMPLETION

For every problem, a self-help book,
for every dry spot, a lotion.

For each kind of flaw, a remedy,
a baguette for each bottle of wine.

A gold ring for each finger,
pearls to grace every neck.

A diet for each over-eater,
a flag for every pole.

For each soldier a salute,
for each undertaker, a corpse.

For every philosopher, a theory,
an explanation of the meaning of life

that inspires college freshmen,
makes sense of it all

until a tornado blows the house off its foundation
or a fuzzy-haired baby is born.

MY DENTIST

Is looking for perfection
in my mouth
and not finding it.

He has an opinion
about every tooth,
its history and condition.

He envisions fresh crowns
created by world-class ceramicists
although he generally uses Americans

because of the exchange rate.
He pictures an all new alignment
created by a dental appliance

worn throughout the night.
A masterpiece could be formed
within my very own mouth

if I weren't so attached
to the thousands it would take
to create it.

You might not know
that crimes of violence
are created by mouths

out of alignment.
You know the guys with rifles
in the tops of school towers?

They were driven there
by misaligned jaws.

TO BE FEMALE

I'm warm and juicy down below
and somewhat sore having been probed
with an inflexible metal tube
to photograph my bladder
which turns out to have no stones.

It brings back the tender vulnerability
of menstrual periods,
emotional water-laden sensitivity.
Should any human part be this soft,
this subject to injury?

I remember that heavy lower back,
the wet pads, like the body crying,
grief-laden blood.
To be female is to bleed.
I tried to convince my daughters
it wasn't a burden.

CERVIX

Numb and dumb,
like the tip of a penis,
but without the feeling.
It's always been
that warm marble
with an eye
at the top of the vaginal canal.
Now collapsed, falling out,
emerging finally
to see the world.

A YOUNG LESBIAN COUPLE

enters the coffee shop.
They sit across from one another
gazing into the other's eyes,
melting in their glow,
their longing.
So geared up inside
they could run marathons
but settle for jiggling
a crossed leg,
bouncing a foot.

The long-haired blonde
sketches her partner,
a brown-skinned Latina.
They can't bear not touching,
reach for hands across the table.
Twenty-four hours of yearning
compressed in twenty minutes.
A few intense words,
then time to catch the bus,
go home to their parents.

MIDDLE-AGED COUPLE

The middle-aged couple
long-married
duck into the coffee shop
out of the rain
he guiding her in
with his tallness
his caring
she smiling back and up to him.

How blissful this trust,
this communion
how protected they are
under this umbrella of concern.

And I wonder
could I ever again
be this unguarded
this caught up in devotion.

OLD FLAME

He drove a red hard-top
convertible. His lips were soft
as figs. I was seventeen.

While he toured Europe for the summer,
I worked as a file clerk saving money
to buy his gift, a Mont Blanc pen.

He wore creased trousers, tailored shirts,
tweed jackets, a monogrammed
needlepoint belt. His erect posture
spoke of military boarding school.

Manners formal enough for royalty,
he said *Pardon my appearance,*
when dressed in jeans
and fraternity sweatshirt.

A subscription to *Time* magazine
was delivered to his college mailbox.
Surely his nails weren't manicured
but they glowed immaculate,
neat and filed. His straightened
white teeth gleamed.

We claimed we were studying
at his parents' home. His aunt
said *Sure you are.*

His skin was my foreign country.
He drew me like a drug.
Me: *What if we go upstairs?*
Him: *I won't be responsible for what happens.*
I knew he spoke the truth.

Sitting with him in the front seat
of his dad's luxury car, the massive
windshield wipers sweeping the expanse
of glass, I thought I would trade my soul
for this life.

While he traveled abroad, I practiced
being sophisticated,
watched myself smoke in the mirror.
I planned carefully what to say
in my airmail notes, trying to make
my life sound interesting. That must
have been the year I read all
the Russian novels.

He wasn't amused by my letters
written on tissue paper. His friends
thought them juvenile.

After this endless summer,
my parents welcomed him
with an elegant homecoming dinner.
Later finally alone with him in his car,
I presented the Mont Blanc pen.
He flushed with modest thanks.

Once he lent me the red convertible,
my girlfriends in the back seat
as I screeched off
and only some guardian angel instinct
halted my impulse to open the roof
as we shot forward
allowing us all to proceed with our lives
more or less intact.

WRINKLES

My face has grown old on me,
showcasing, without permission,
my age.
And it's obvious for all to see—
unless I adopt a burka.

And then I try to remember
it doesn't matter your place
on the labyrinth.
Each location equally real
and valid,
one spot not superior
to another.

Fully inhabit this space,
without regret, longing.

LONGING FOR HALE-BOPP

We got used to the watching
straining our necks
having it part of our lives.

We grew accustomed to enchantment
together in the night air
watching its path silent and sure
across the black sky
sodium tail streaming,
festive as the Fourth of July.

We knew it was on a journey,
a signpost into blue infinity
before disappearing forever
through a sieve of time.

Still somehow we got attached
wanting it to go on forever
within our sight
these last months of our innocence
before your diagnosis.

Even now
after all these years
still I gaze at the night sky
longing for Hale-Bopp.

INK

I'm funny about my pens.
I used to write only with a real
fountain pen
until they became a nuisance
with their incessant leaks.
Now,
I use only a rollerball
preferably with a micro point
but fine will do in a pinch.

What I absolutely won't use—
the lowly ballpoint.
I can't tell you the times
I've had a pen leak
all over my hands
writing a check in church
or I remember Ellen
at M. D. Anderson
desperate to get ink stains
off her fingers
on her way to treatment
needing to feel worthy
of being healed.

CONFIRMATION

All dressed up
girls in dresses and sandals
boys in dress shirts and slacks
all clean and shiny
smiling for the cameras
age 14
with their rounded shoulders
anticipation of so much weight
already there.

UNATTAINABLE

The slick glossy magazine

with pictures of exotic places—
white robed men in Morocco—

bazaars in Istanbul—
gondolas in Venice—

appeared to my young eyes
as fairy tales beyond reach,

as out of place
in our unvarnished home

as fine china
in a diner.

I asked my Dad
why he subscribed

when these were places
we'd never go.

He said
for you.

REFRAIN

I

Every time I drive by Second
and Ormsby, I catch a glimpse
of my growing adolescent self
climbing the marble stairs
of this tall-ceilinged Victorian
house, my father by my side.

We were welcomed by Mr. Sims,
my elderly piano teacher,
who lived alone.
I remember him tall and thin
with fragile skin, delicate hands.

My father stayed reading
in a straight-backed chair
in the entryway
while Mr. Sims and I proceeded
to the parlor's black upright piano.

He sat by my side as I plunked along,
hard slick keys
under my fingers,
notes reverberating down
long empty corridors.

Encouraging me to practice,
be grateful for these lessons,
he seemed sad when I left,
as though this was the only
life that breathed in these hollow dark rooms.
I departed to find my father sitting there
attending, loyal, with me.

II

And now I wait outside a door,
overhead fluorescent lights,
halls filled with kids
dancers in leggings,
laughter echoing.

My granddaughter of the glossy red hair
inside with her brightness,
learning the whole notes, half notes,
playing with aplomb,
singing with assurance,
bubbling her way through a Friday.

She exits the lesson, all smiles,
and we bounce together
down the steps, into the car
and belt out all the way home
Tomorrow, Tomorrow, I love you
Tomorrow, you're always a day
away.

AT CROSS COUNTRY MEET

All those adolescent boys at the starting line
bright singlets and shorts
lined up alert for the starting gun
and then off in a flash
thundering past us this early fall day,
blue-skied crisp and cool.

They stream past—a blast of color,
running all out
as though their lungs may burst.
By the end, they're salty with sweat.
The boys run for the team, run
for themselves, run as though
their life depends on it.

As they start, tears well up,
stream down my face uncontrolled,
uncontrollable.

Why does this move me so deeply?
What do they embody for us—
how hard they try, what can
a human endure?

All our desires, hopes for the future
packaged in this DNA.
Parents, grandparents line the course,
wet grass coating our shoes—
GO, GO, GO—

FROM MY PORCH IN THE HIGH RISE

Far from, yet close to my protected high rise—
matters of life and death.

> Two men standing in a fishing boat
> haul large carp out of the river.

They're efficient in black rubber overalls,
red kerchiefs tied around their heads.

> Wearing brown gloves,
> hand over hand, they pull in the net.

With lightning reflexes, they throw it out,
then drag it back in loaded with fish.

> Pitching out driftwood, trash—they toss
> their catch in the bottom of the boat.

The vessel soon heavy—30 or 40 two feet long,
white bellies stained red—flopping, gasping.

> I sit with my binoculars,
> dishwasher humming in the background.

SUMMER SOLSTICE II

I wake before the alarm
saturated in light,
68 degrees early morning on the river
creamy clouds overhead.
The river waveless and shining—
but around it the engines of commerce,

a distant train, tracks rumbling,
a highway's unending traffic.
The world vibrates with sound,
but this great waterway still and silent.

THE OTTER

It took so long to identify her—
coming as she does in the almost-dark,
and small as she is in the distance.

She scampers,
        pours herself
in and out of the lake
like mercury.

Could there be a liquid being?

On land, she's a running comma,
a lump in her back as she lopes
across the green.

Appearing as she does
only in the half light—
she's a creature bridging worlds:

Night and day—water and land.

Only now that I've identified her,
am I almost sure she's not a mythical being.

In full daylight I wonder if I imagined it:
slithering serpent-like from one pond to another.
What would she feel like to touch?

Wet fur with warmth underneath,
like my dog frisking out of the lake.

PEDESTRIANS

Waddling across the yard
in late afternoon shadows
heads down vigilant
a pair of female mallards.

What do they seek
squat to the ground
travelling on thin orange legs?

CAVE HILL ONCE AGAIN

I got here early after all the times
of just driving by. I arrived after

a proper shower and clean clothes
so I'd be worthy of being here.

Plastic flowers and a flag on your grave.

I rip them out and throw
them in my trunk.

Too bad I can't be here full-time
to protect you.

You'd say they meant well
and forgive them.

Early morning shadows grace
your tomb, mid-summer green

lushness. I'm already considering
what's next on my schedule.

Do I remember you or only
remember remembering you?

Palpable the force field
of protection of your love.

I'm turning into an old person
here before my eyes. I raise

my arm, move it in pantomime
as though in a dance.

I come here to honor you,
set aside this time.

SELF-CARE

She knew I loved myself
by how I stroked my belly—
a sight glimpsed from the bathroom
that first night we spent together.
She saw a view of me I thought unseen,
an action I wasn't aware of,
although I know I sometimes stroke my arm
ever so lightly so I can barely feel
the arm hairs stand on end.

Now I know enough to know
when I need to retreat into meditation,
stop to observe the fleeting thoughts,
watch my body as it sits aging in place.

MEDITATIONS ON THE VIETNAM WALL

As the walkway descends,
the black marble walls etched
with the names of the dead
grow taller, surrounding us
with more and more names.
We are being buried by the dead—
taken over by this epic loss.

Then there are the crowds
interacting with the wall,
leaving behind candles, teddy bears, notes.
People kneeling, hands on a name,
humans bereft.

Cold stone with the power
to unloosen torrents of tears,
deep wells of sorrow.

COLLEGE BASEBALL TEAM ON THE PLANE

Easy smiles and joking,
the air around them crackles,
forearms muscular,
veins protruding,
faded jeans hardly
contain what bulges beneath.

With one hand, each tosses
a canvas bag in the overhead.

Athletic strides—
all coiled power.
The military can't wait
to have them sign
on the dotted line.
Fodder for our foes.

BOARDING SCHOOL AT PEBBLE BEACH

The gardener, brown-skinned,
rakes pine needles,
a light scratching on dry ground.
It must feel good on the earth's back.

I sit on a bench
absorbing the sunshine,
the pine fragrance,
contemplating what it's like
to breathe the priciest air
in America.

The gardener, whistling,
wears a dusky blue cap
with a frayed bill.
Twice his annual salary
wouldn't pay one child's tuition.

Sun filters through the pines,
baptizing all in its path.

REIFICATION

A quick fix to the terrifying anxiety of living
in a vast dark world: we put in a box
all power and then pray to it,
never acknowledging that nothing
in the universe is separate
from anything else.
Nothing stands alone, unpermeated.

ELKHORN FERN

I'm beginning to feel a little
fenced in by the fern.
Massive and shaggy, the size of a small bison,
or a Volkswagen bug,
sadly cut down along with my live oak,
now ensconced next to my sliding door,
still alive thanks to the watering system.

It grows bigger every day.

I fear it's morphing into Audrey II
and will soon block my view
and grow with seeking vines
right into my house.
It's sucking up all the oxygen
and sending out tentacles
for something else to eat.

I shiver when our eyes meet.
I've started using another door.

SAPLING

I can't wait to see the first bird in my new tree—
a creature looking for a place to perch.

So far, this sapling stands too fragile,
and tentative, leaves feathery, delicate.

Could it even support a sparrow?
A cormorant wouldn't even try.

How will the tree feel? Like a horse
being ridden? Invaded?

Or spacious and accommodating,
coming into its own as a host to the world,

part of the giving and receiving
of all living beings.

COTTONWOOD TREE

The cottonwood tree outside my window
is joyous—leaves quivering in ecstasy,
shaking like cheerleader pom-poms.
If they made a sound
it would be cymbals, tympani,
sharp blast of trumpets—
the exhilaration of a marching band
against a deep blue sky,
confetti falling all around.

Despite all this movement,
the cottonwood stands still,
thirsty roots reaching
toward the river.

Its trunk, massive and weathered,
one deep gash, a record
of major storms, lightning or disease.
The leaves are thinning now
as fall approaches,
like the elderly with their fragile
skin and hair.

Dignified, it holds
its branches high
in tribute to the life
it's lived, in tribute to the sky.

AFTER MY UNTIMELY DEATH

Sometimes as I leave the house
I foresee people coming in and finding
remains of my life spread out like the ruins
of Pompeii. For sure on the floor
my Birkenstocks, well-worn and embedded
with my DNA, journals, books and magazines
stacked by my chair, yesterday's running shoes
beneath the table, shoestrings dangling,
toothbrush standing at attention, maybe the towel
still damp, a coffee cup with the final dregs,
today's New York Times spread out,
half read.

Did I leave a light still burning,
awaiting my return? The chairs
around the table askew,
a life in process, my fuzzy lap
blanket still on the footstool,
housing my sloughed-off cells
hiding out in the folds of the yarn,
fingerprints on the sliding door
belong to this particular life.

Thoughts and dreams religiously recorded,
black ink in journal after journal,
stacks of them. Shelves of books
underlined and notated, my sweat
smudged on each page. Light streams
in through the blinds as usual.

Funny, all the years of viewing Orion's Belt,
I thought my place on earth
was permanent.

ABOUT THE AUTHOR

Pat Owen went from the left-brain career of legal publishing to the right-brain world of poetry. The shift still sometimes makes her dizzy. Her work has appeared in *The Louisville Review,* the *Gulf Stream Literary Magazine* and the anthologies *This Wretched Vessel, & Grace,* and *The Messenger Is Sudden Thunder.* She was a finalist in the *Atlantic Review International Poetry Competition.* Her debut poetry collection, *Crossing the Sky Bridge* was published by Larkspur Press.